GRAPHIC LIBRARY

GRAPHIC SCIENCE

ADVENTURES IN SOUND

WITH MAX AXIOM SUPER SCIENTIST

An Augmented Reading Science Experience

by Emily Sohn | illustrated by Cynthia Martin and Anne Timmons

Consultant:
Dr. Ronald Browne
Associate Professor of Elementary Education
Minnesota State University, Mankato

CAPSTONE PRESS
a capstone imprint

Graphic Library is published by Capstone Press,
1710 Roe Crest Drive, North Mankato, Minnesota 56003.
www.mycapstone.com

Library of Congress Cataloging-in-Publication Data is available on the Library of
Congress website.

ISBN: 978-1-5435-2944-9 (library binding)
ISBN: 978-1-5435-2955-5 (paperback)
ISBN: 978-1-5435-2965-4 (eBook PDF)

Summary: In graphic novel format, follows the adventures of Max Axiom as
he explains the science behind sound.

Art Director and Designer
Bob Lentz

Colorist
Michael Kelleher

Cover Artist
Tod Smith

Editor
Christopher L. Harbo

Photo Credits

Capstone/Scott Thoms: 8; Capstone Studio/Karon Dubke: 29

Download the Capstone app!

- Ask an adult to download the Capstone 4D app.

- Scan the cover and stars inside the book for additional content.

When you scan a spread, you'll find fun extra stuff
to go with this book! You can also find these things
on the web at www.capstone4D.com using the
password: sound.29449

TABLE of CONTENTS

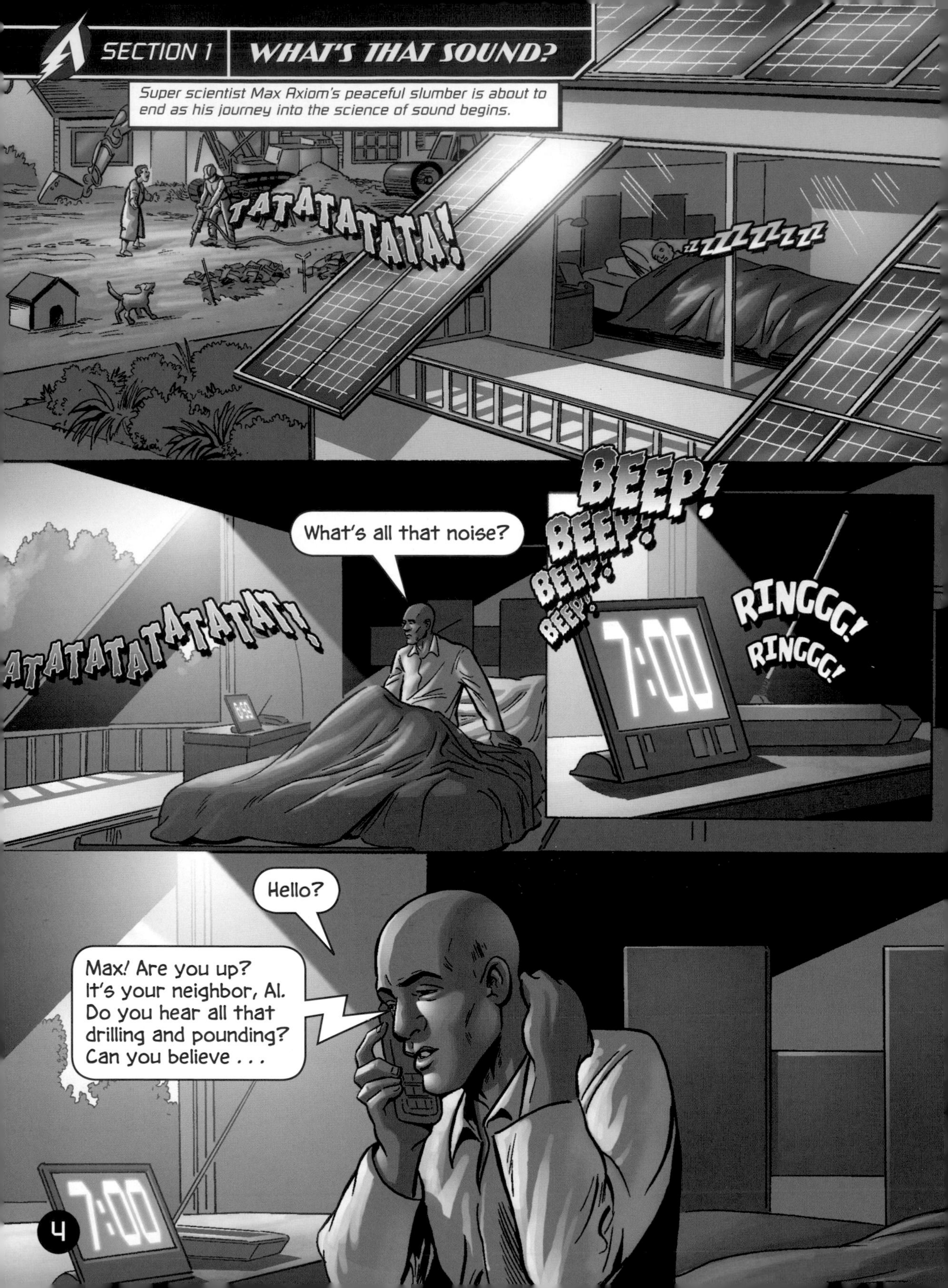
SECTION 1
WHAT'S THAT SOUND?
Super scientist Max Axiom's peaceful slumber is about to end as his journey into the science of sound begins.
TATATATATATA!
ZZZZZZZZ
What's all that noise?
ATATATATATATATAT!
BEEP! BEEP! BEEP! BEEP!
7:00
RINGGG! RINGGG!
Hello?
Max! Are you up? It's your neighbor, Al. Do you hear all that drilling and pounding? Can you believe . . .
7:00

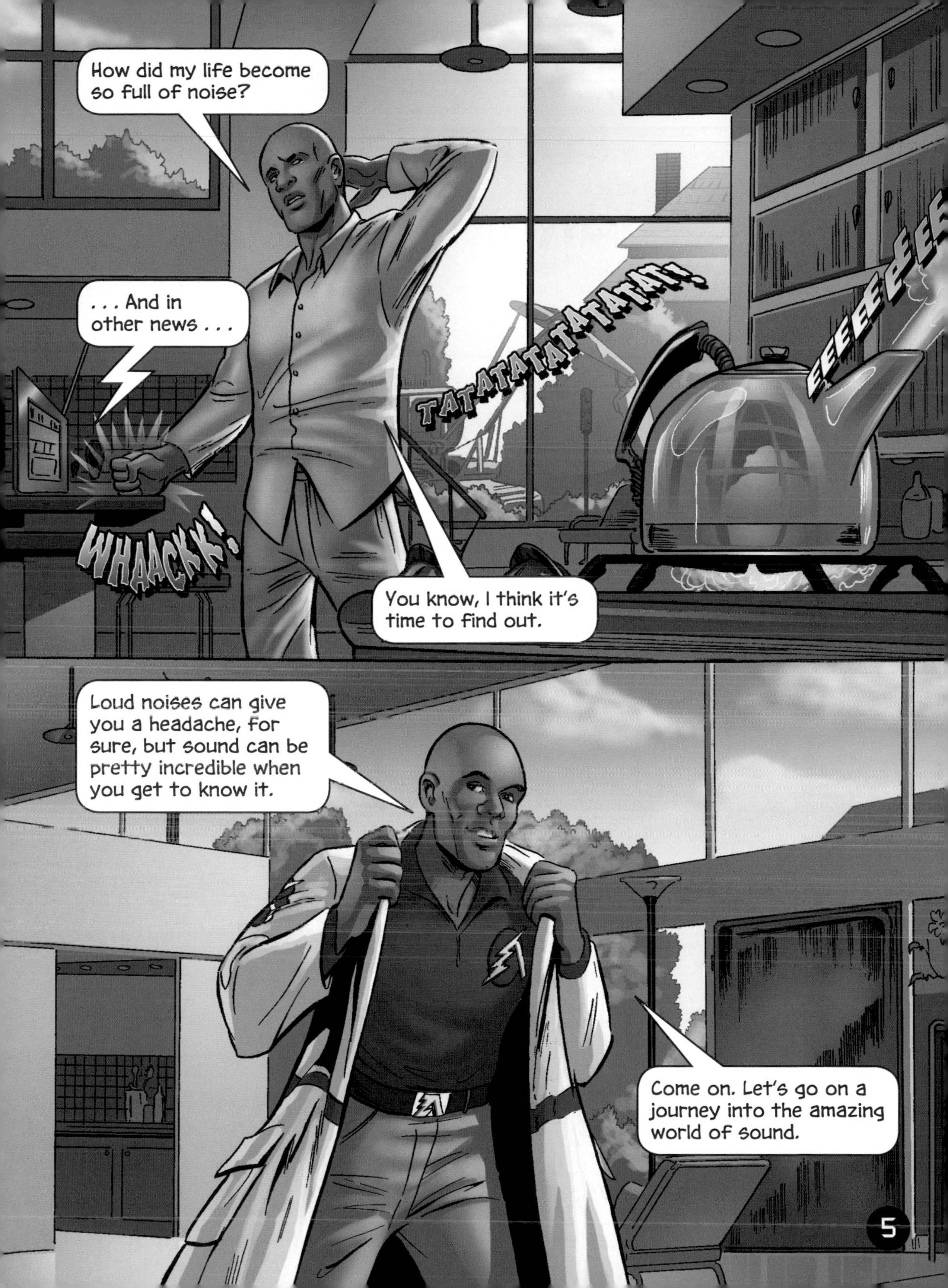
How did my life become so full of noise?
. . . And in other news . . .
WHAACKK!!
TATATATATATATATAT!!
EEEEEEEEE
You know, I think it's time to find out.
Loud noises can give you a headache, for sure, but sound can be pretty incredible when you get to know it.
Come on. Let's go on a journey into the amazing world of sound.

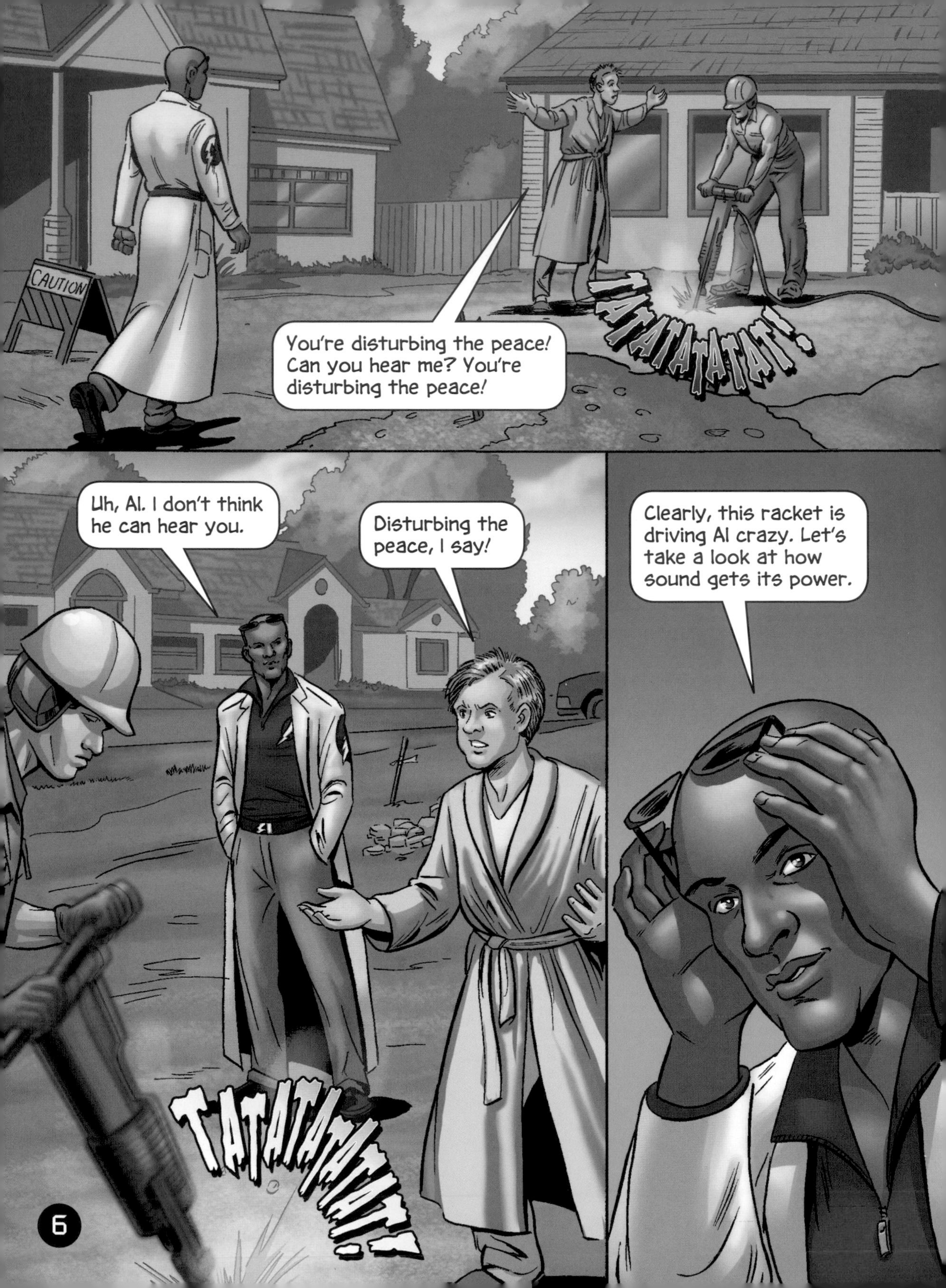
CAUTION
You're disturbing the peace! Can you hear me? You're disturbing the peace!
TATATATATATAT!
Uh, Al. I don't think he can hear you.
Disturbing the peace, I say!
TATATATATAT!
Clearly, this racket is driving Al crazy. Let's take a look at how sound gets its power.

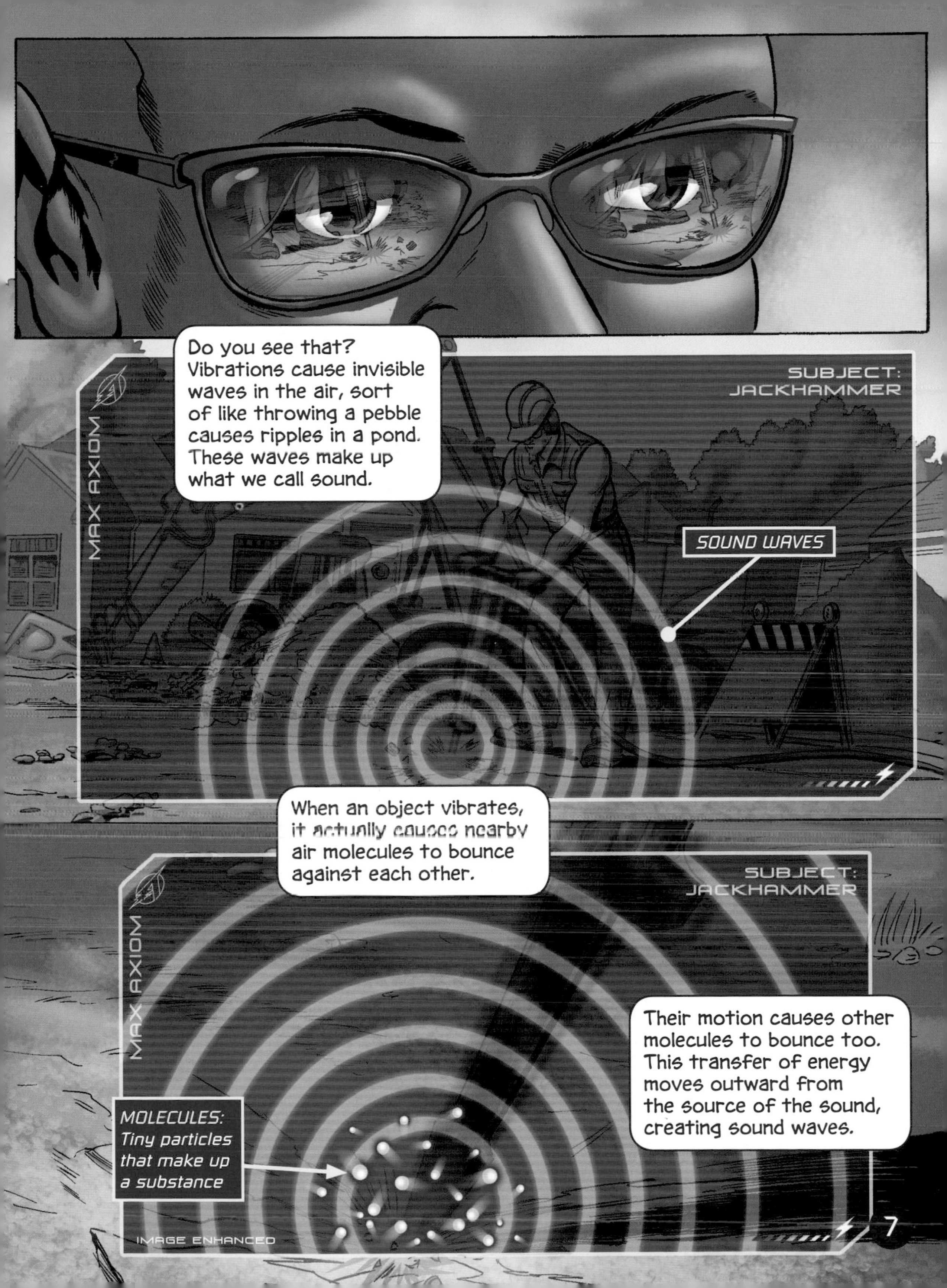
Do you see that? Vibrations cause invisible waves in the air, sort of like throwing a pebble causes ripples in a pond. These waves make up what we call sound.
MAX AXIOM
SUBJECT: JACKHAMMER
SOUND WAVES
When an object vibrates, it actually causes nearby air molecules to bounce against each other.
MAX AXIOM
SUBJECT: JACKHAMMER
Their motion causes other molecules to bounce too. This transfer of energy moves outward from the source of the sound, creating sound waves.
MOLECULES: Tiny particles that make up a substance
IMAGE ENHANCED

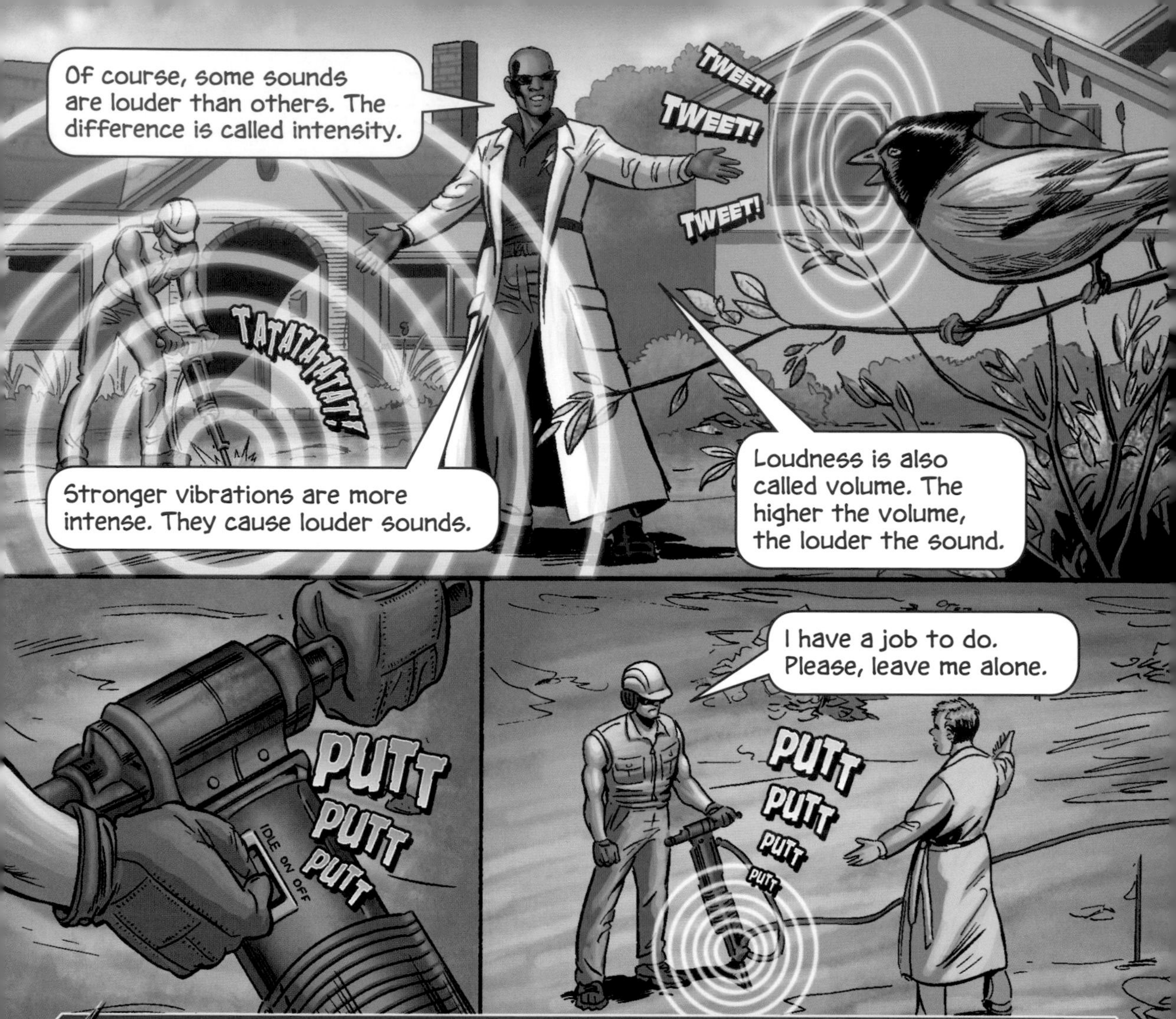
Of course, some sounds are louder than others. The difference is called intensity.
TWEET!
TWEET!
TWEET!
TATATATATATAT!
Stronger vibrations are more intense. They cause louder sounds.
Loudness is also called volume. The higher the volume, the louder the sound.
PUTT
PUTT
PUTT
IDLE ON OFF
I have a job to do. Please, leave me alone.
PUTT
PUTT
PUTT
PUTT

THE HUMAN LARYNX

ACCESS GRANTED: MAX AXIOM

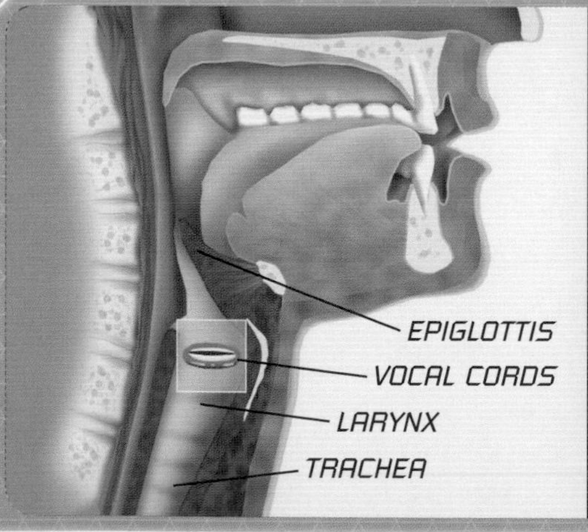
EPIGLOTTIS
VOCAL CORDS
LARYNX
TRACHEA

Inside your throat, your larynx allows you to talk, sing, and make other noises. Inside the larynx, two muscles called vocal cords squeeze together and vibrate as air passes by them. The faster they vibrate, the higher your voice sounds. Your tongue and lips shape the sounds you make.

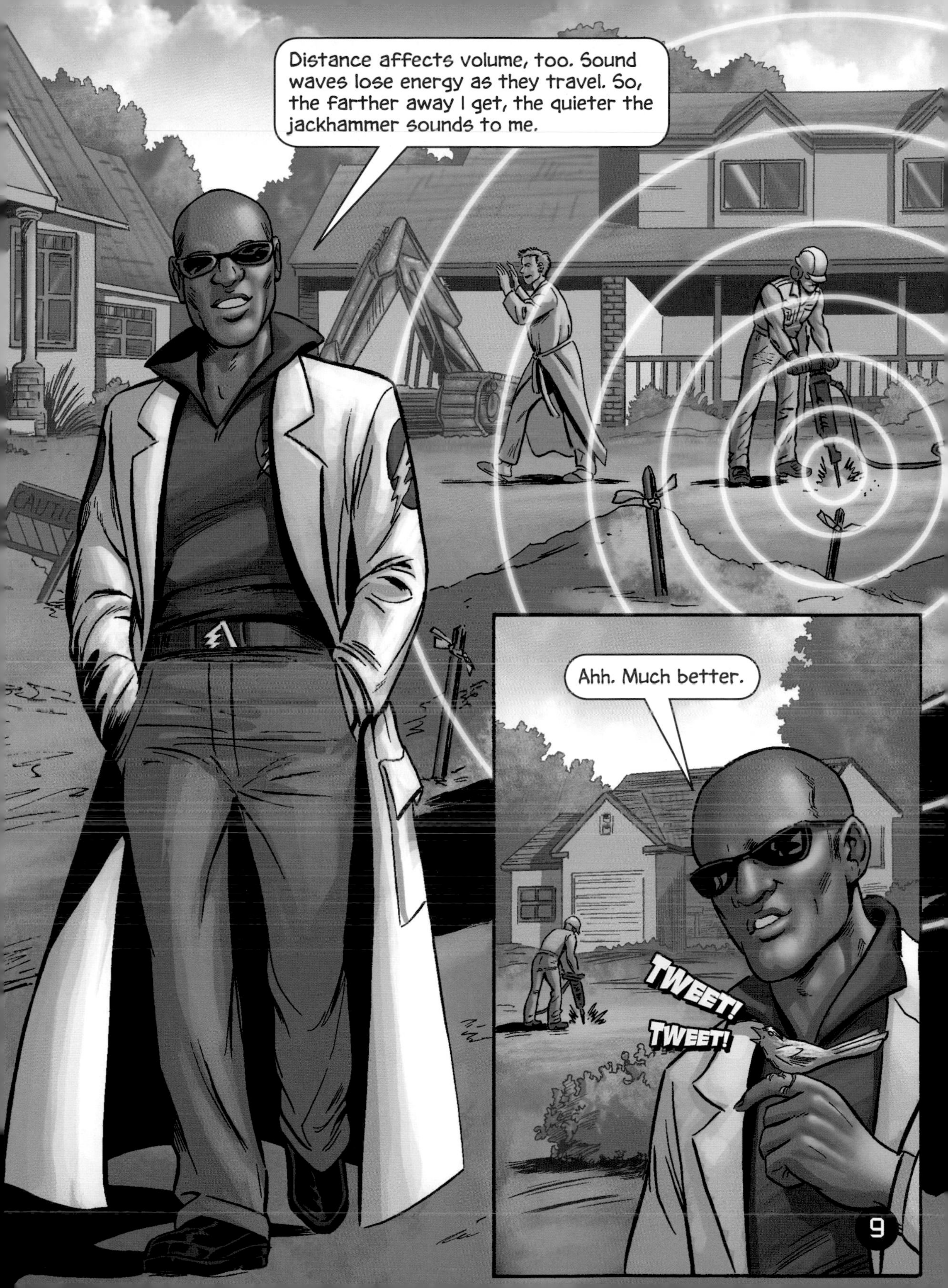
Distance affects volume, too. Sound waves lose energy as they travel. So, the farther away I get, the quieter the jackhammer sounds to me.
CAUTION
Ahh. Much better.
TWEET!
TWEET!

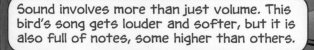

Sound involves more than just volume. This bird's song gets louder and softer, but it is also full of notes, some higher than others.

The bird may not know it, but the secrets behind its lovely melody are called frequency and pitch.

Frequency equals the number of sound waves that pass a point during a certain amount of time.

For instance, right now only one sound wave passes by me each second. Therefore, the sound has a frequency of 1 hertz (Hz).

One Second

But if 50 waves pass by me in one second, the sound has 50 Hz. Faster vibrations create sounds with higher frequencies.

One Second

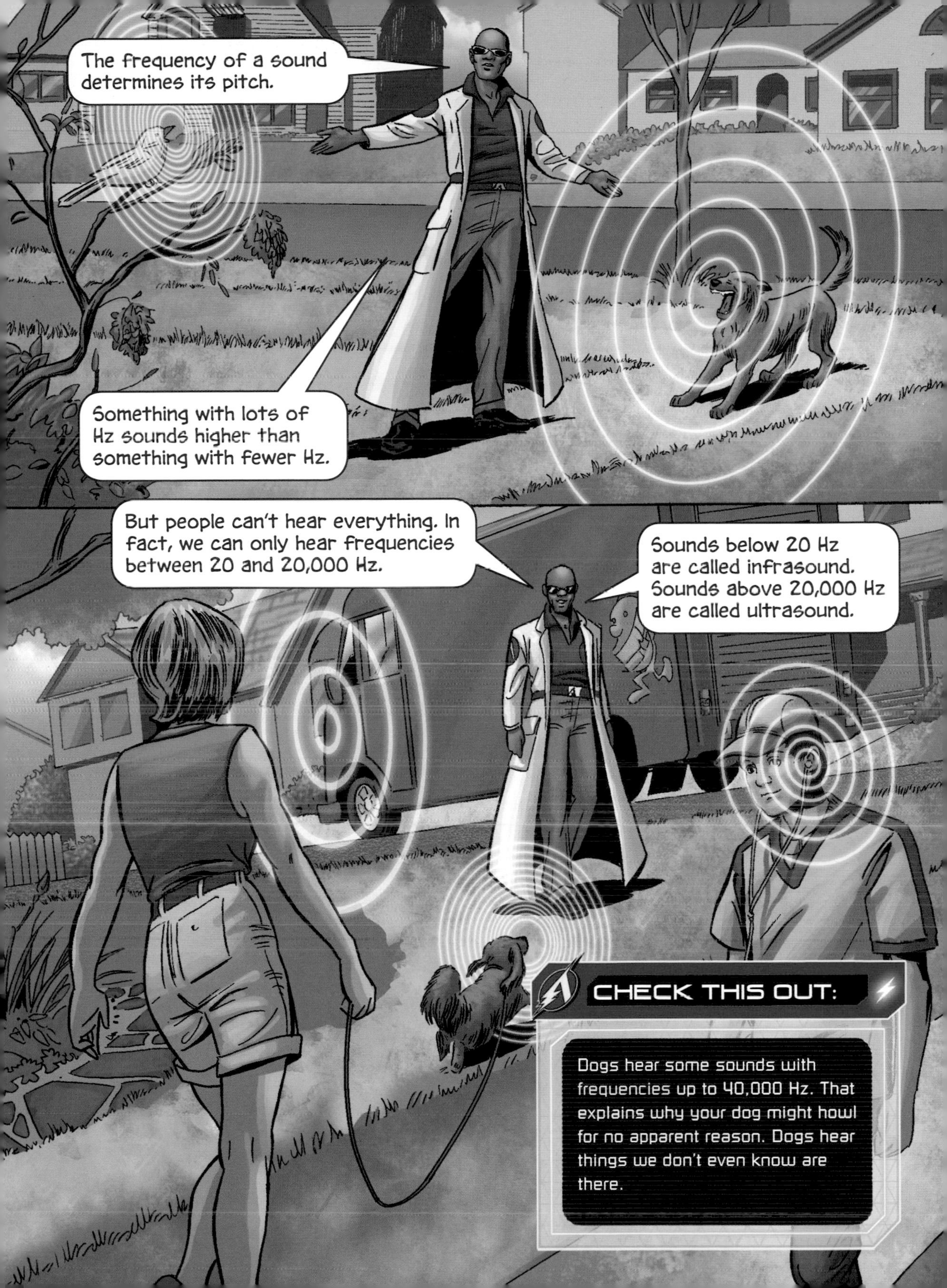
The frequency of a sound determines its pitch.
Something with lots of Hz sounds higher than something with fewer Hz.
But people can't hear everything. In fact, we can only hear frequencies between 20 and 20,000 Hz.
Sounds below 20 Hz are called infrasound. Sounds above 20,000 Hz are called ultrasound.
CHECK THIS OUT:
Dogs hear some sounds with frequencies up to 40,000 Hz. That explains why your dog might howl for no apparent reason. Dogs hear things we don't even know are there.

SECTION 2 MAKING SENSE OF THE WAVES

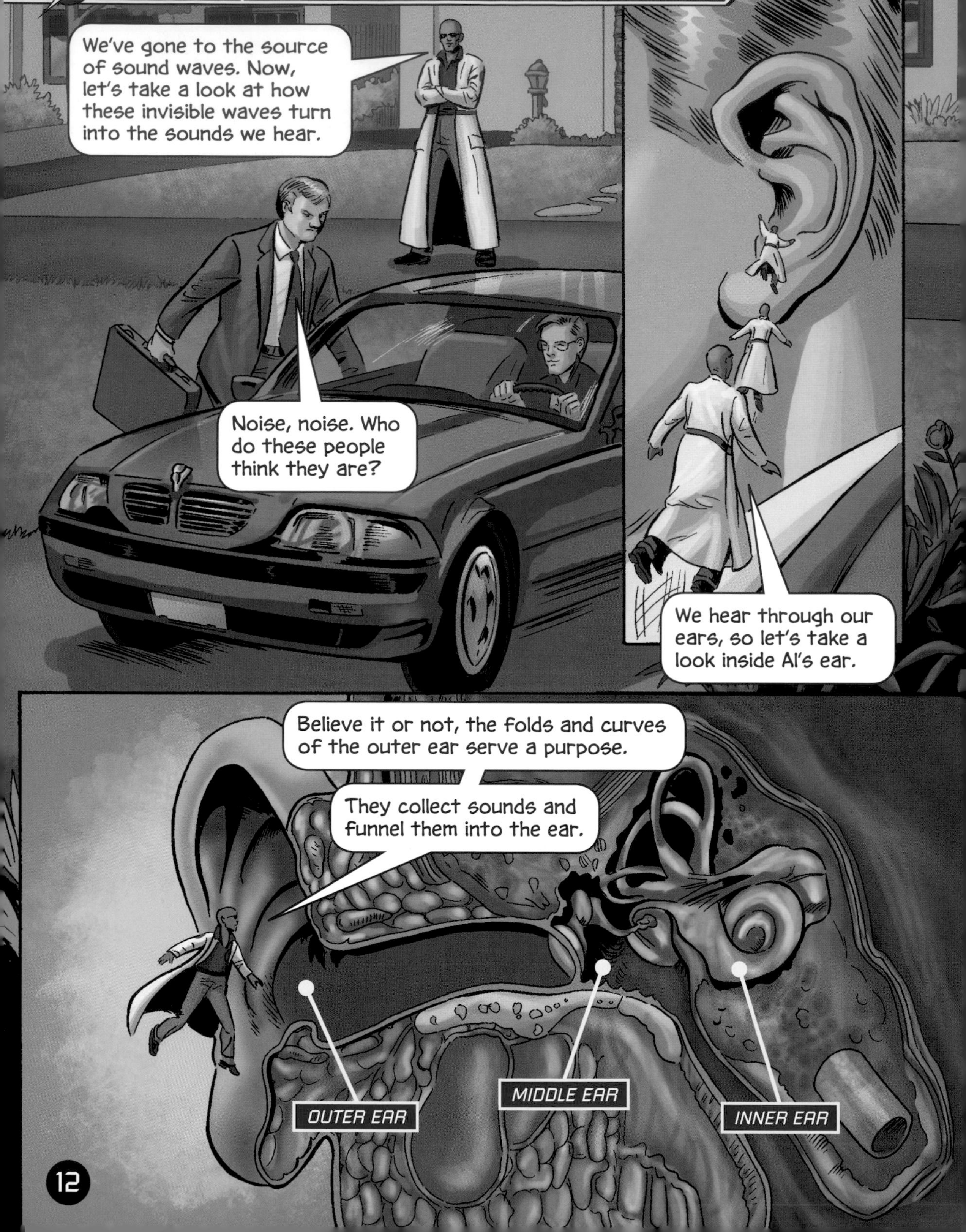
We've gone to the source of sound waves. Now, let's take a look at how these invisible waves turn into the sounds we hear.
Noise, noise. Who do these people think they are?
We hear through our ears, so let's take a look inside Al's ear.
Believe it or not, the folds and curves of the outer ear serve a purpose.
They collect sounds and funnel them into the ear.
MIDDLE EAR
OUTER EAR
INNER EAR

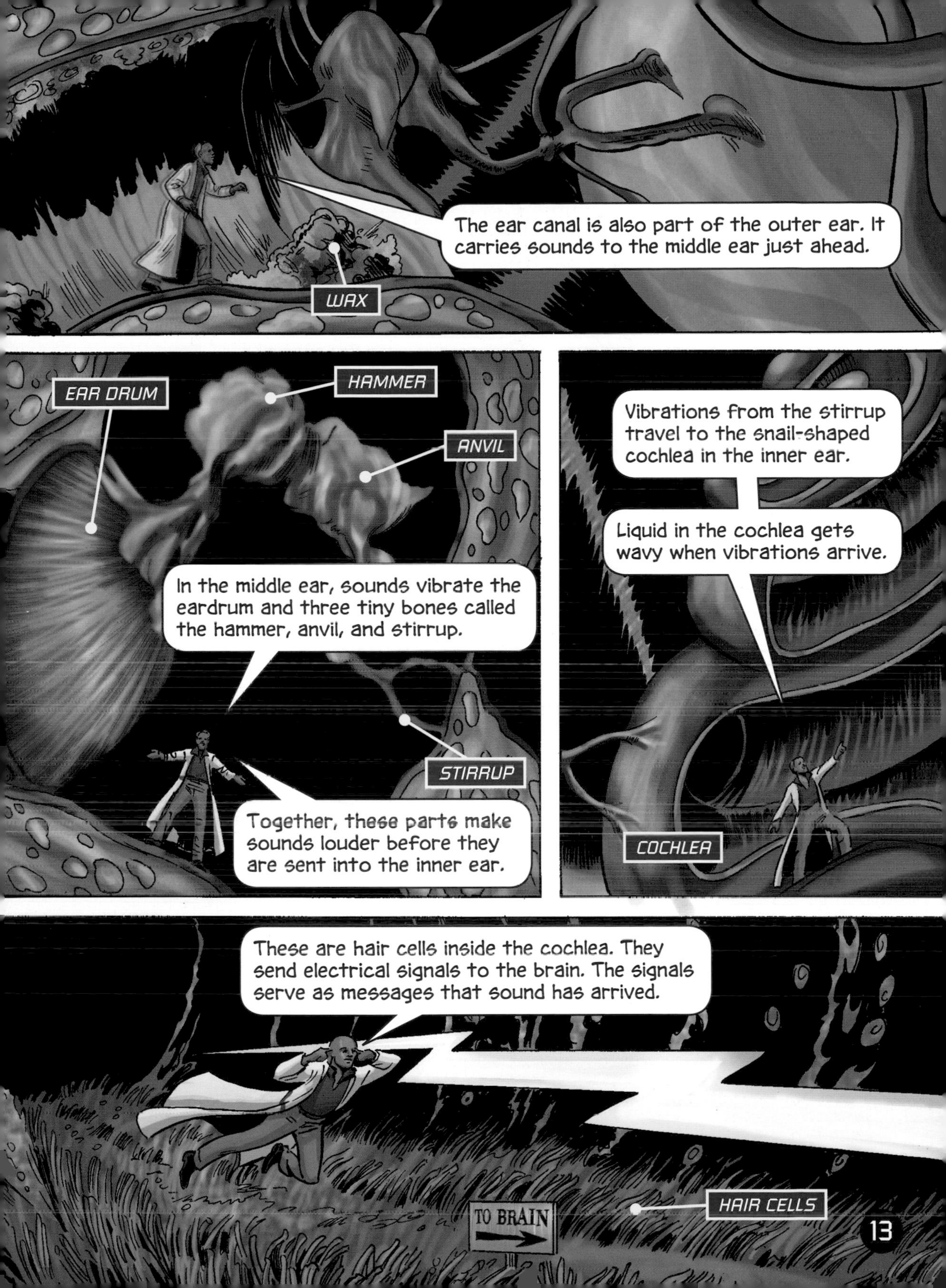
The ear canal is also part of the outer ear. It carries sounds to the middle ear just ahead.
WAX
EAR DRUM
HAMMER
ANVIL
In the middle ear, sounds vibrate the eardrum and three tiny bones called the hammer, anvil, and stirrup.
STIRRUP
Together, these parts make sounds louder before they are sent into the inner ear.
Vibrations from the stirrup travel to the snail-shaped cochlea in the inner ear.
Liquid in the cochlea gets wavy when vibrations arrive.
COCHLEA
These are hair cells inside the cochlea. They send electrical signals to the brain. The signals serve as messages that sound has arrived.
TO BRAIN
HAIR CELLS

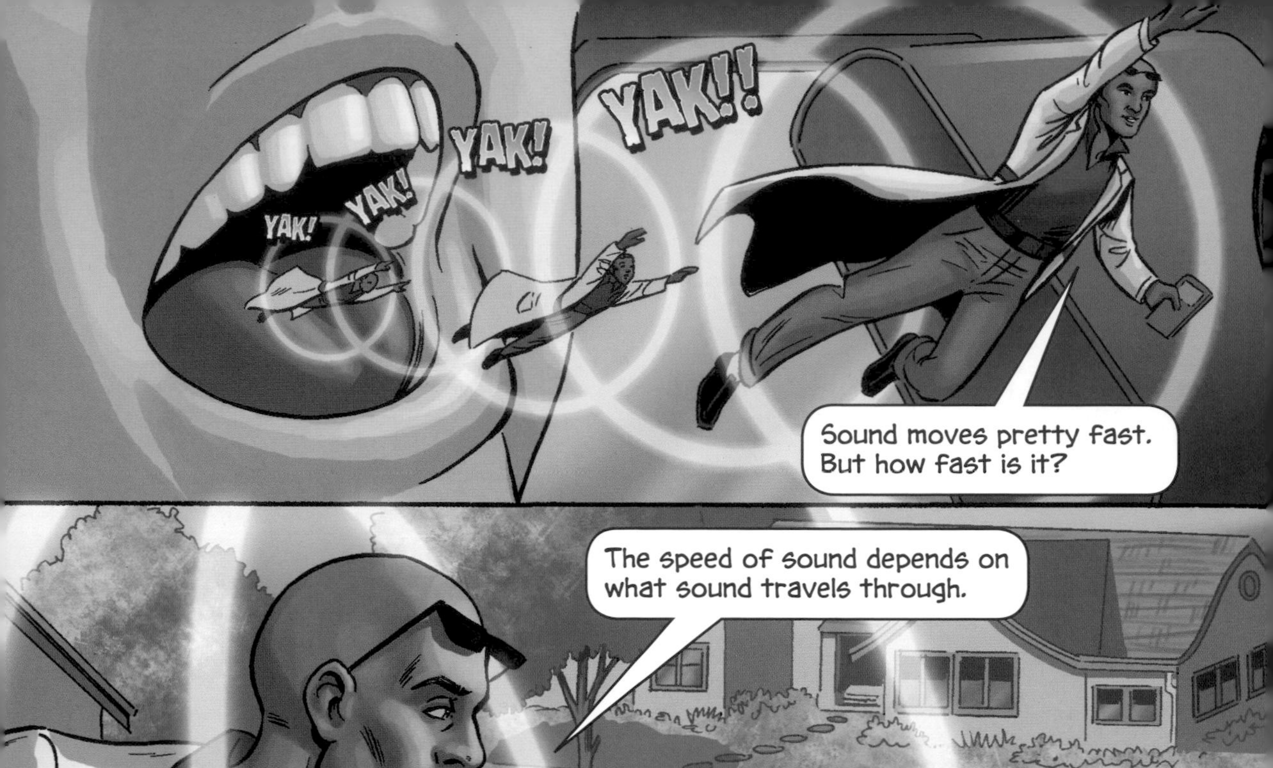
YAK!
YAK!
YAK!
YAK!!
Sound moves pretty fast. But how fast is it?
The speed of sound depends on what sound travels through.
770 MPH
770 MPH
Sound traveling through air at sea level and room temperature moves at 770 miles per hour.

SOUND VERSUS LIGHT

ACCESS GRANTED: MAX AXIOM

In a race, light would leave sound in the dust. Nothing moves faster than light, which zings along at about 670,000,000 miles per hour.

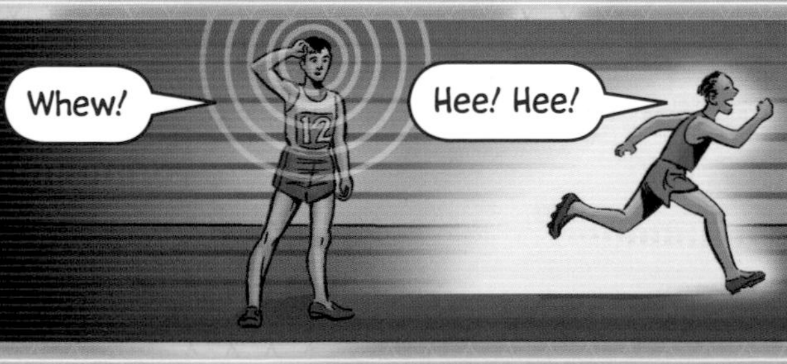
Whew!
Hee! Hee!
12

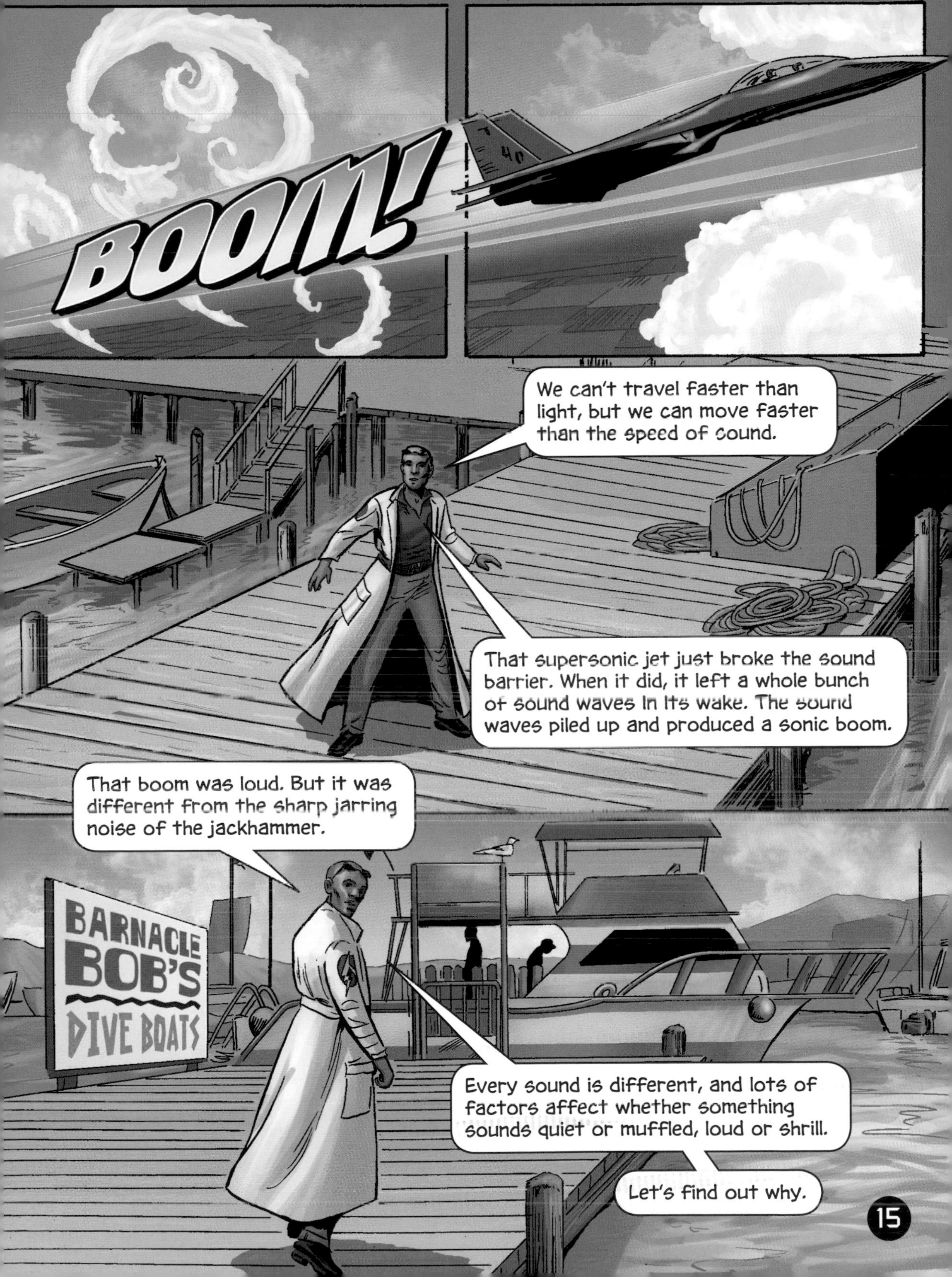
BOOM!
We can't travel faster than light, but we can move faster than the speed of sound.
That supersonic jet just broke the sound barrier. When it did, it left a whole bunch of sound waves in its wake. The sound waves piled up and produced a sonic boom.
That boom was loud. But it was different from the sharp jarring noise of the jackhammer.
BARNACLE BOB'S DIVE BOATS
Every sound is different, and lots of factors affect whether something sounds quiet or muffled, loud or shrill.
Let's find out why.

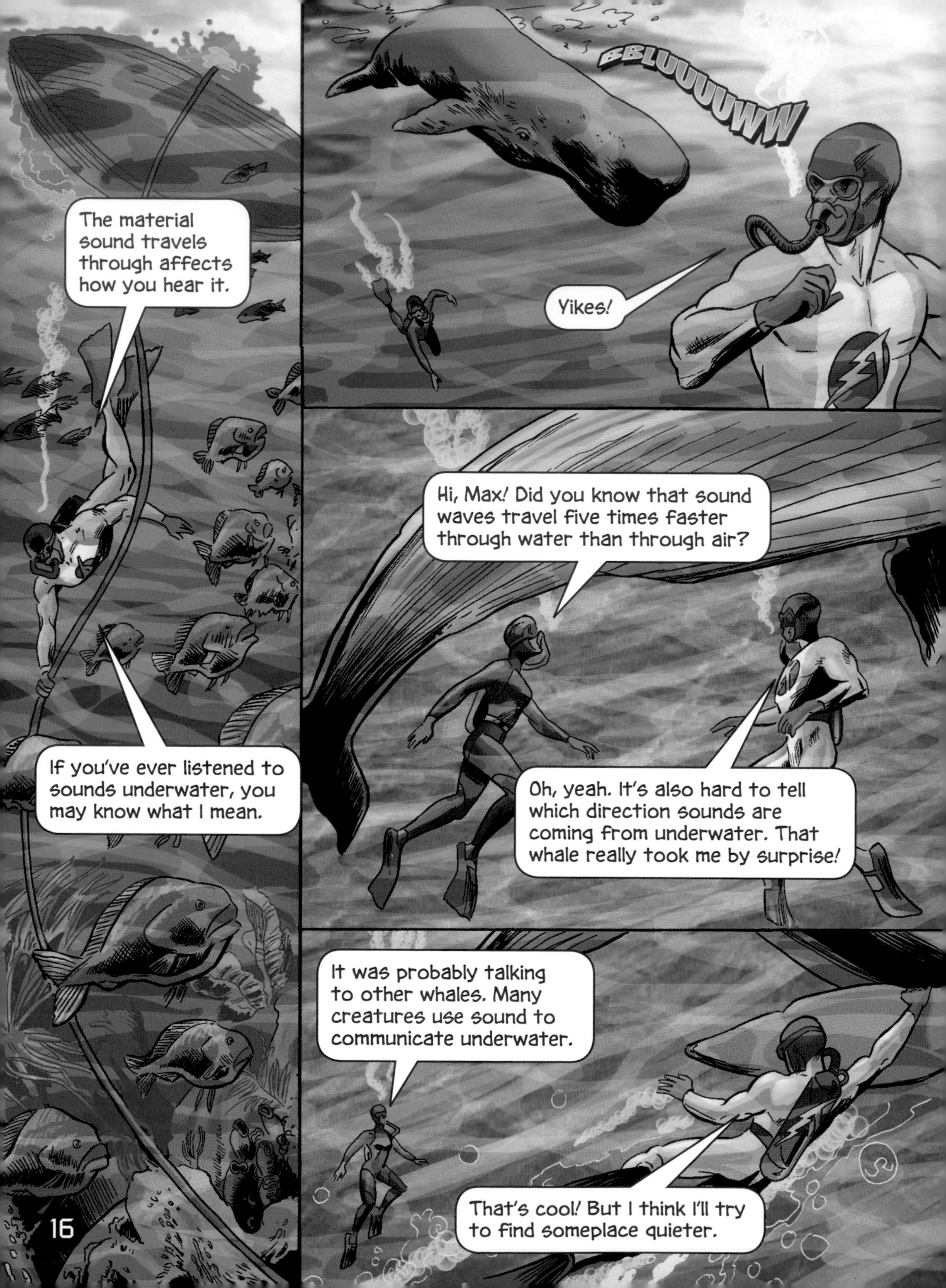
The material sound travels through affects how you hear it.
If you've ever listened to sounds underwater, you may know what I mean.
BBLUUUUUWW
Yikes!
Hi, Max! Did you know that sound waves travel five times faster through water than through air?
Oh, yeah. It's also hard to tell which direction sounds are coming from underwater. That whale really took me by surprise!
It was probably talking to other whales. Many creatures use sound to communicate underwater.
That's cool! But I think I'll try to find someplace quieter.

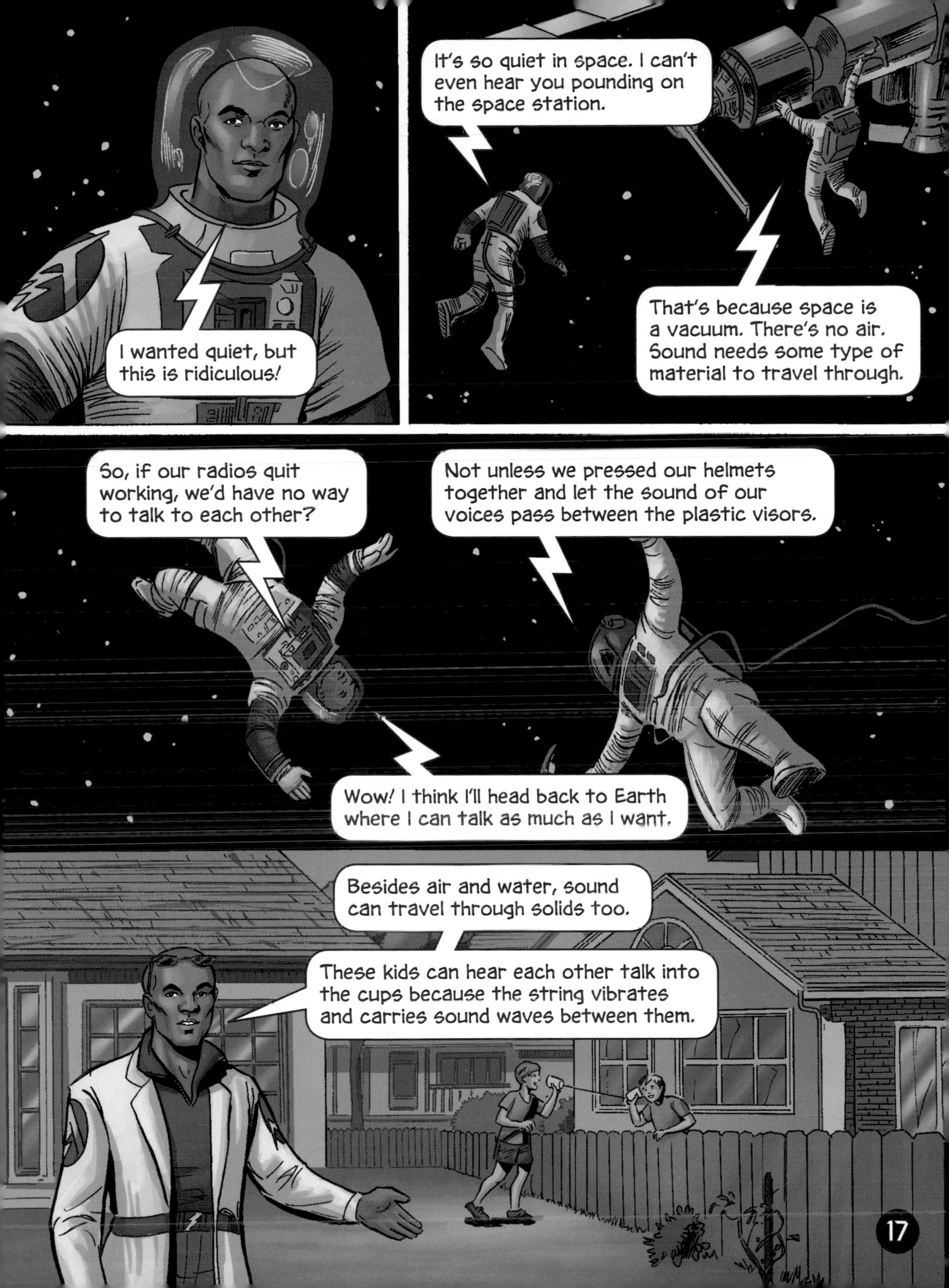
I wanted quiet, but this is ridiculous!
It's so quiet in space. I can't even hear you pounding on the space station.
That's because space is a vacuum. There's no air. Sound needs some type of material to travel through.
So, if our radios quit working, we'd have no way to talk to each other?
Not unless we pressed our helmets together and let the sound of our voices pass between the plastic visors.
Wow! I think I'll head back to Earth where I can talk as much as I want.
Besides air and water, sound can travel through solids too.
These kids can hear each other talk into the cups because the string vibrates and carries sound waves between them.

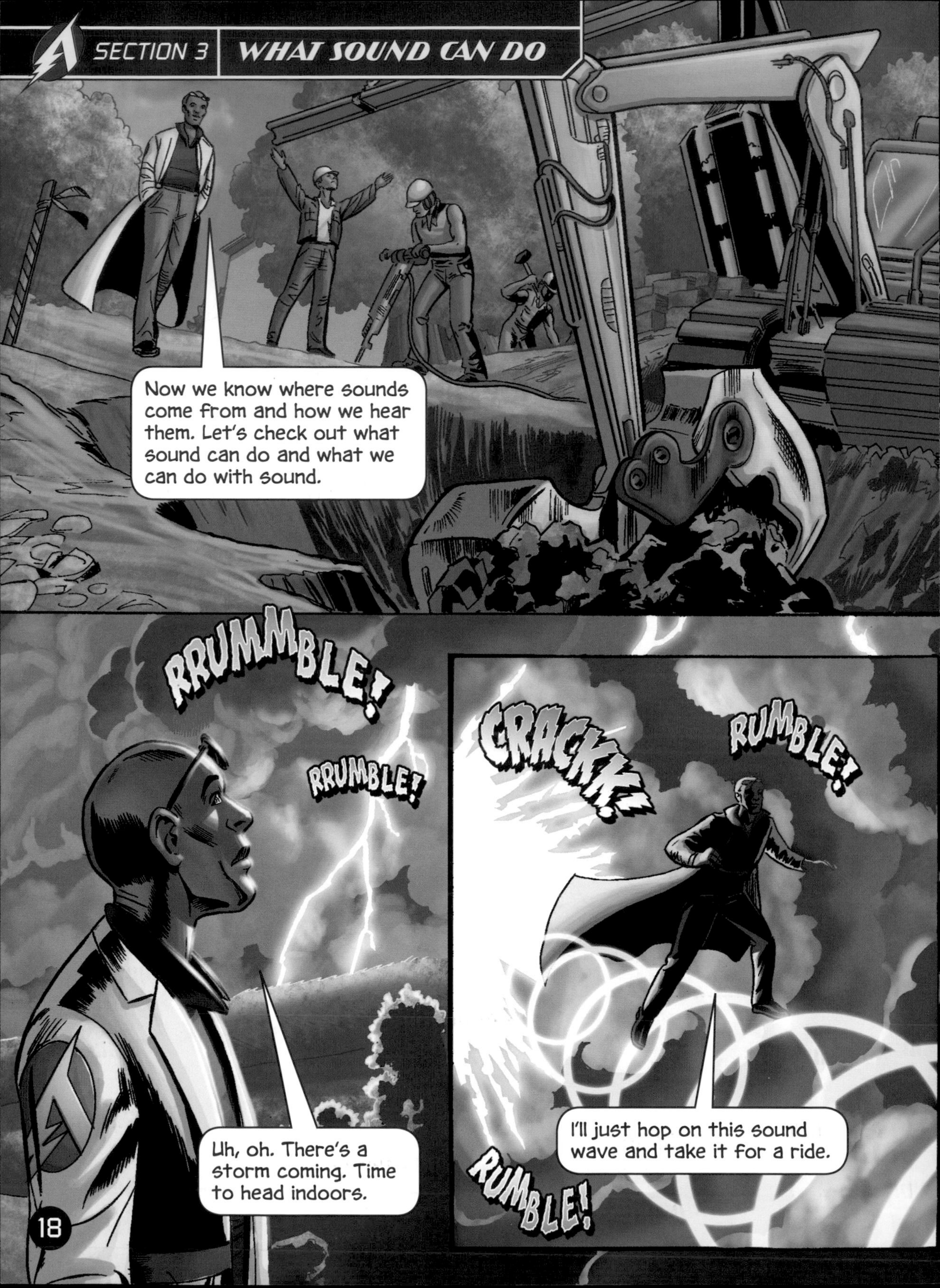
Now we know where sounds come from and how we hear them. Let's check out what sound can do and what we can do with sound.
RRUMMBLE!
RRUMBLE!
Uh, oh. There's a storm coming. Time to head indoors.
CRACKK!
RUMBLE!
I'll just hop on this sound wave and take it for a ride.
RUMBLE!

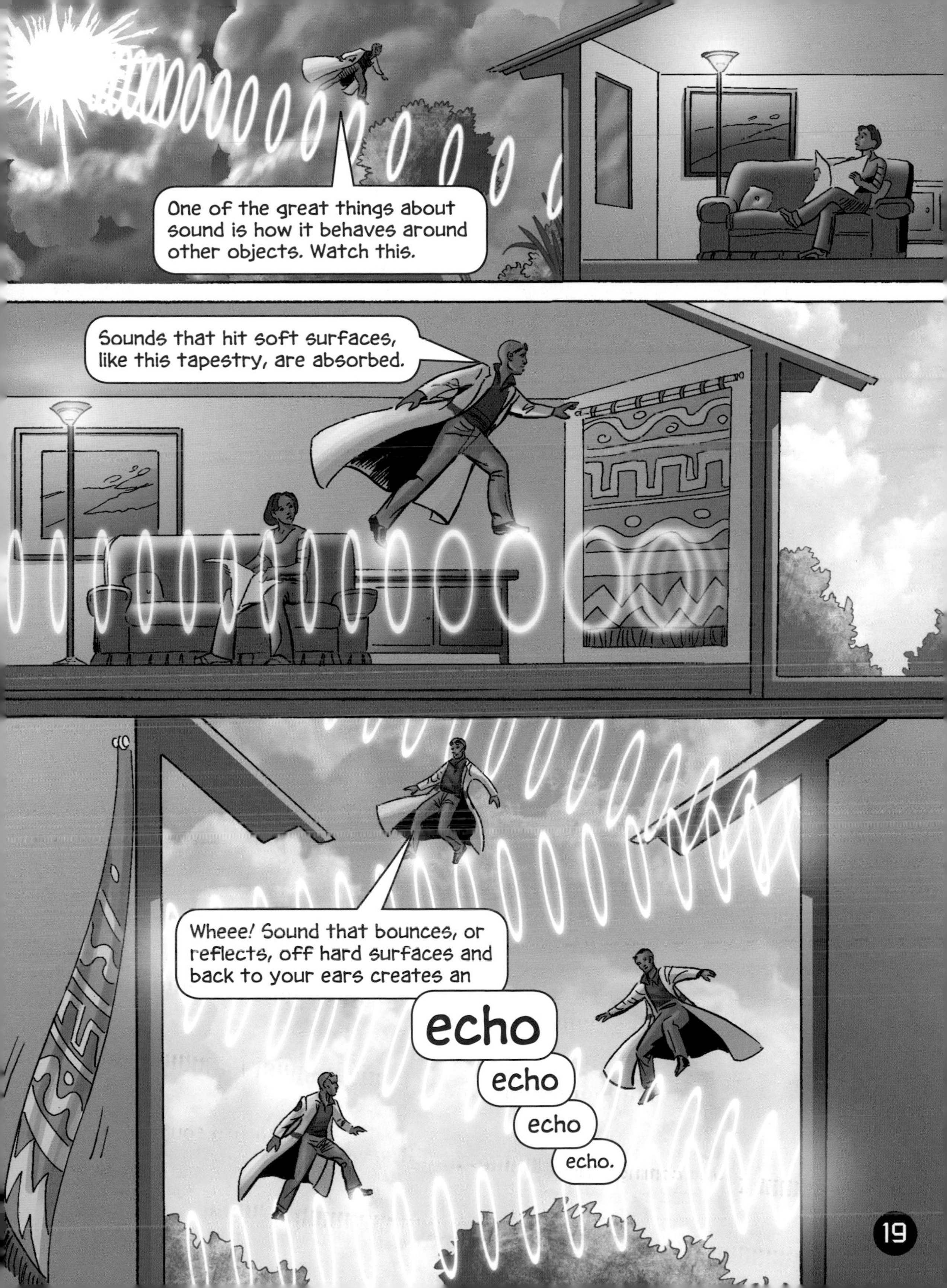
One of the great things about sound is how it behaves around other objects. Watch this.
Sounds that hit soft surfaces, like this tapestry, are absorbed.
Wheee! Sound that bounces, or reflects, off hard surfaces and back to your ears creates an
echo
echo
echo
echo.

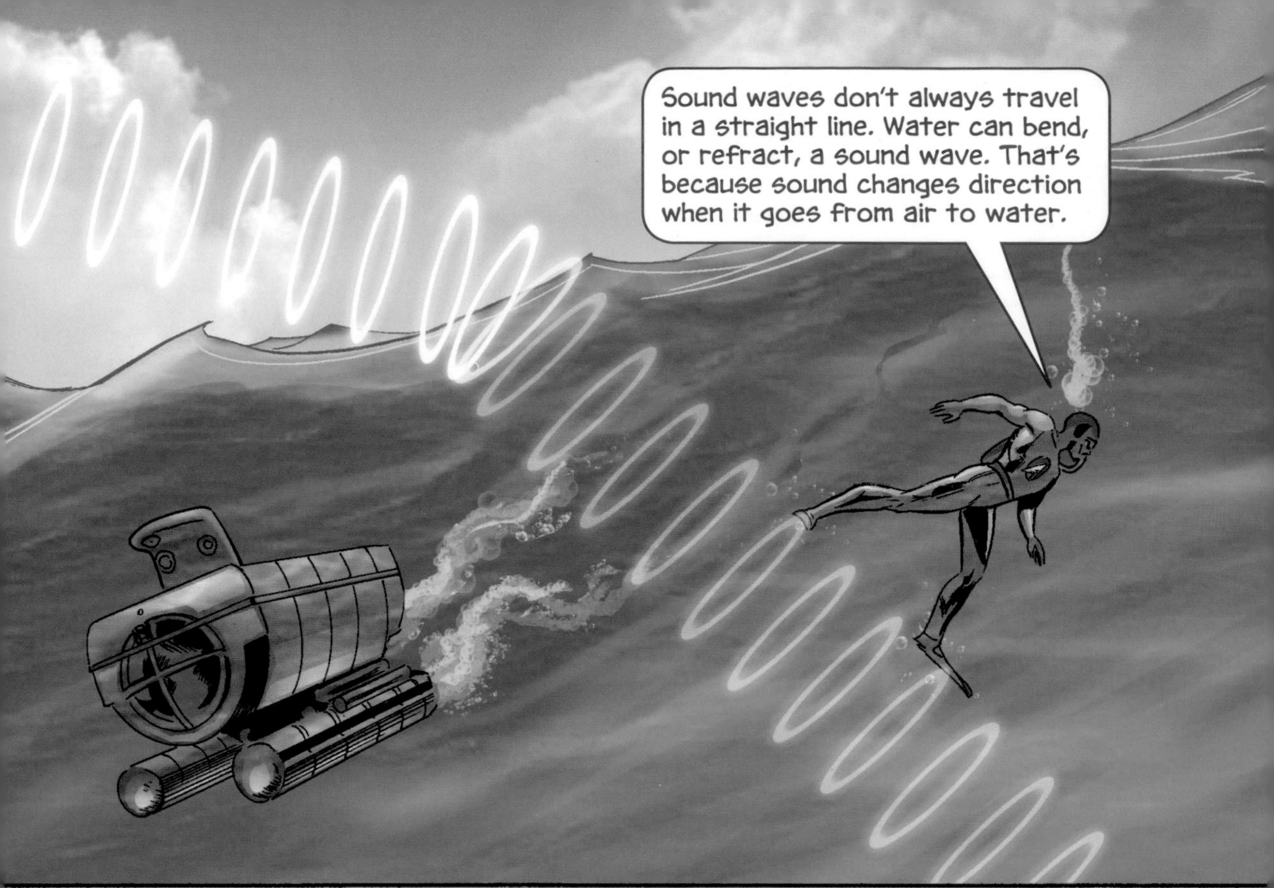
Sound waves don't always travel in a straight line. Water can bend, or refract, a sound wave. That's because sound changes direction when it goes from air to water.

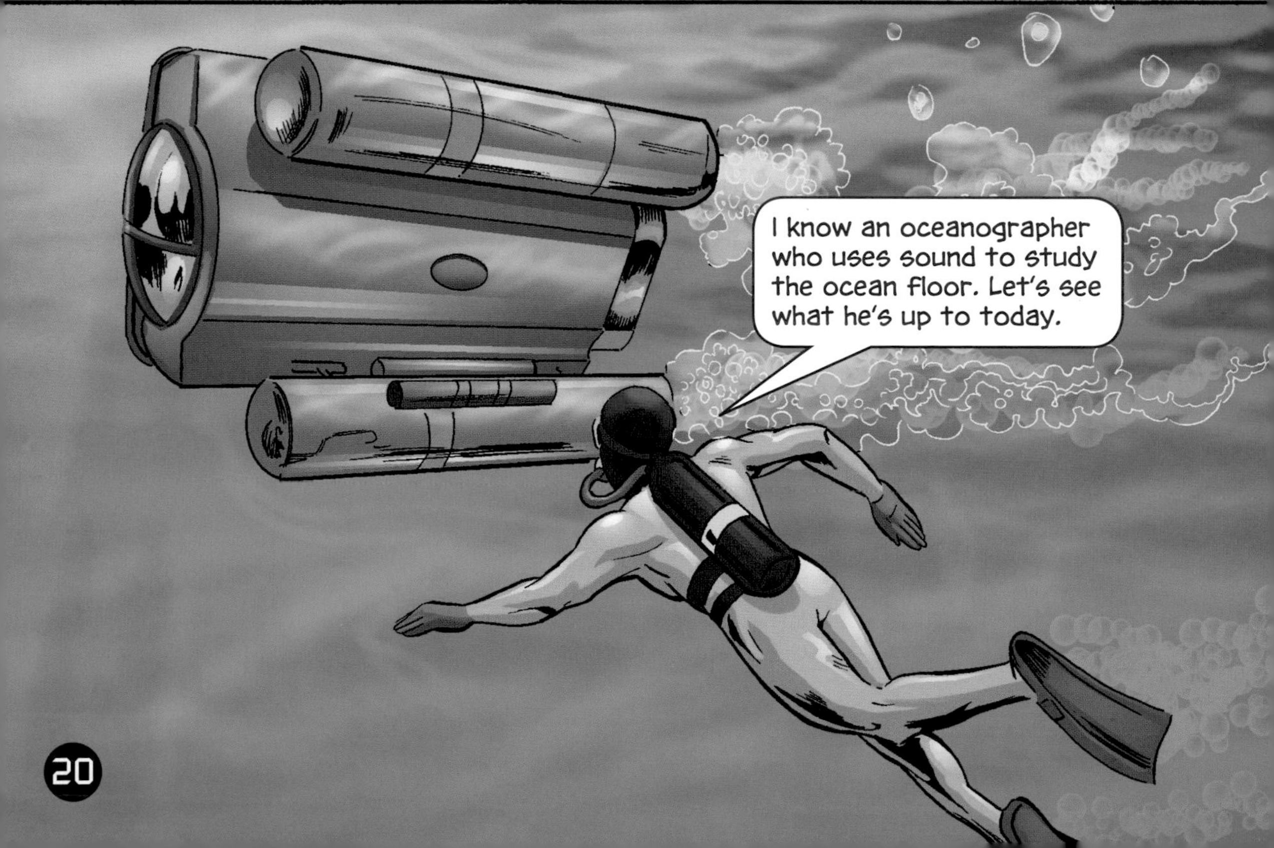
I know an oceanographer who uses sound to study the ocean floor. Let's see what he's up to today.

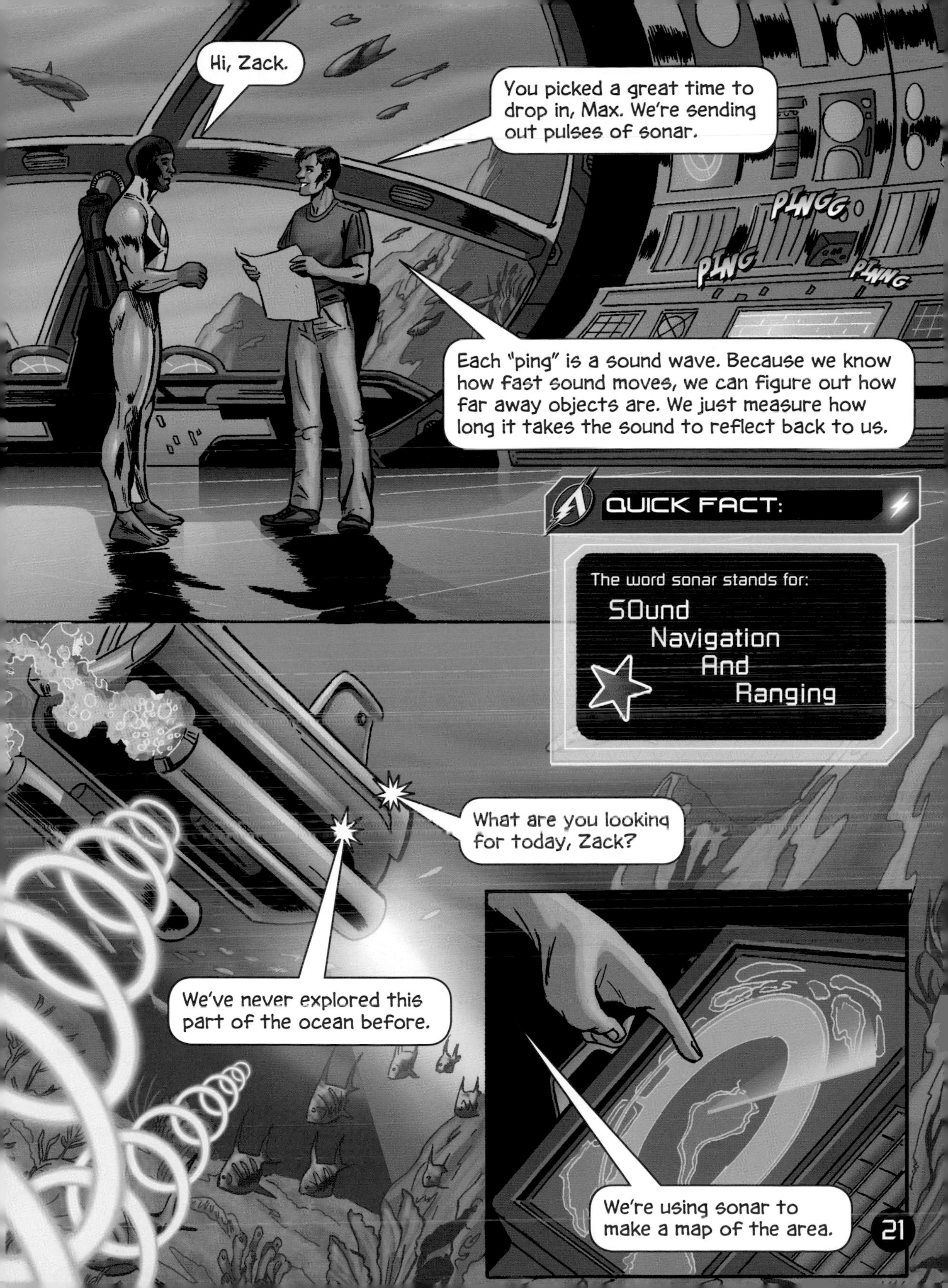

Hi, Zack.
You picked a great time to drop in, Max. We're sending out pulses of sonar.
PINGG
PING
PINNG
Each "ping" is a sound wave. Because we know how fast sound moves, we can figure out how far away objects are. We just measure how long it takes the sound to reflect back to us.
QUICK FACT:
The word sonar stands for:
SOund
Navigation
And
Ranging
What are you looking for today, Zack?
We've never explored this part of the ocean before.
We're using sonar to make a map of the area.

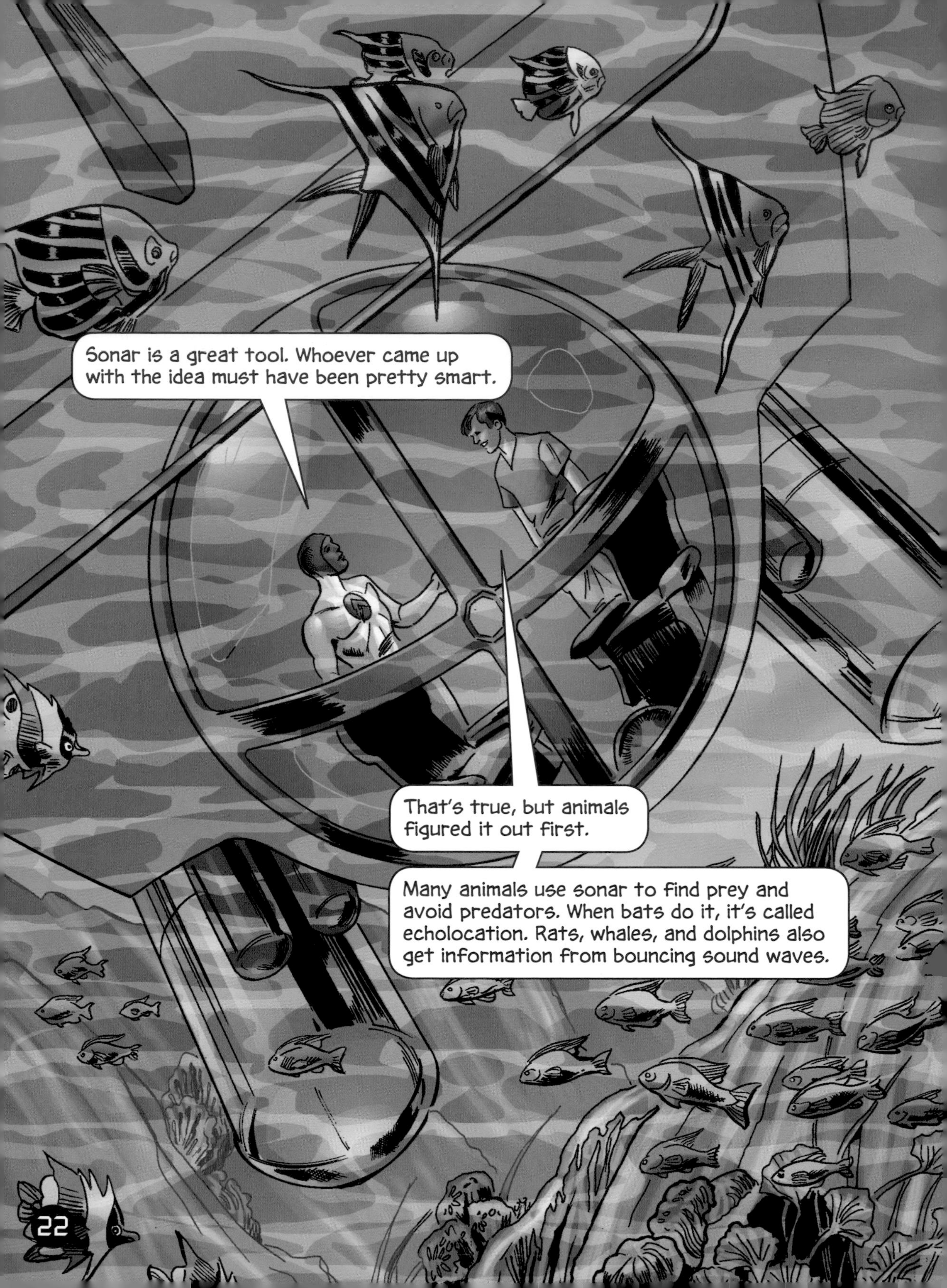
Sonar is a great tool. Whoever came up with the idea must have been pretty smart.
That's true, but animals figured it out first.
Many animals use sonar to find prey and avoid predators. When bats do it, it's called echolocation. Rats, whales, and dolphins also get information from bouncing sound waves.

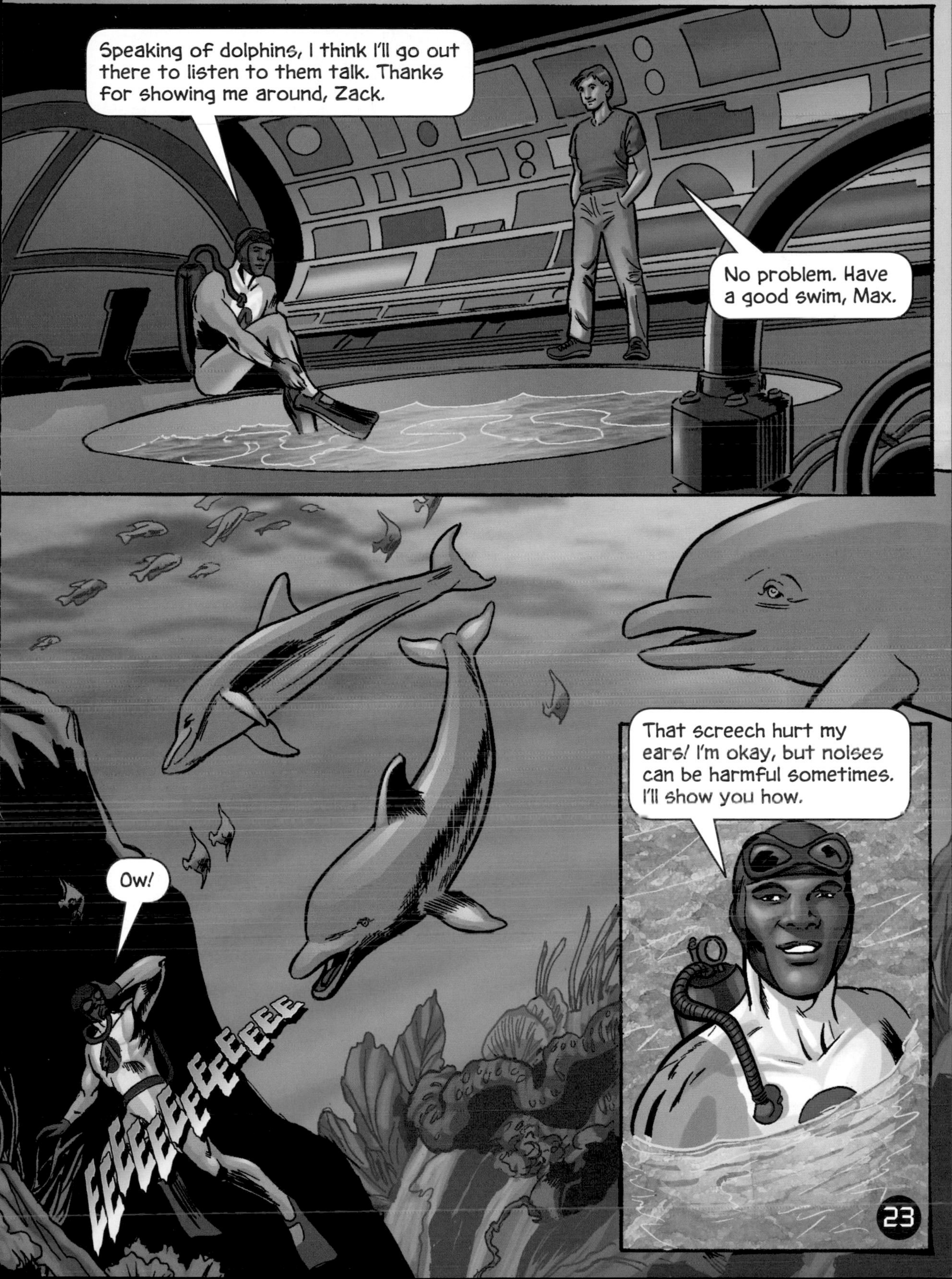
Speaking of dolphins, I think I'll go out there to listen to them talk. Thanks for showing me around, Zack.
No problem. Have a good swim, Max.
Ow!
EEEEEEEEEEEEEE
That screech hurt my ears! I'm okay, but noises can be harmful sometimes. I'll show you how.

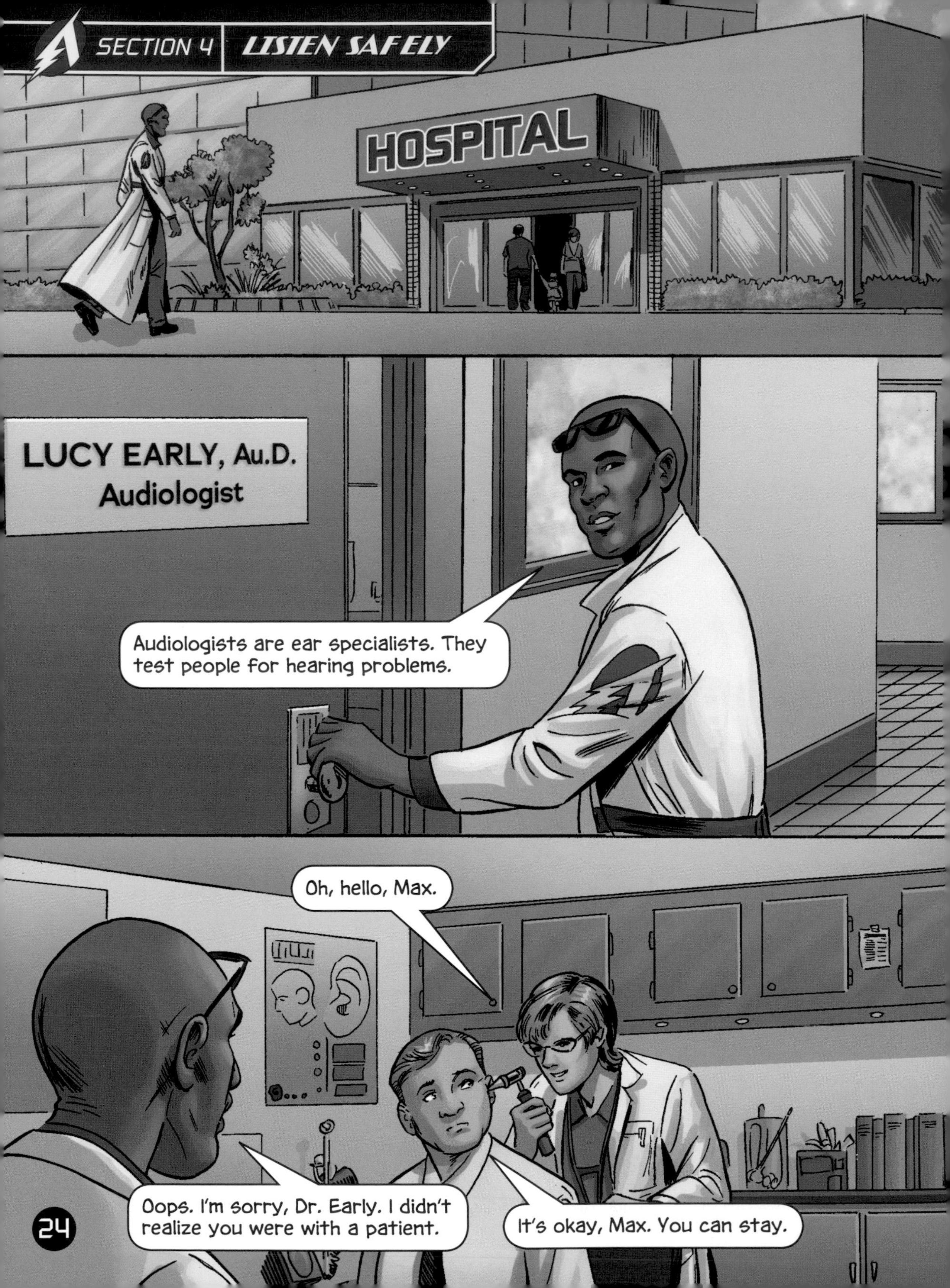
HOSPITAL
LUCY EARLY, Au.D.
Audiologist
Audiologists are ear specialists. They test people for hearing problems.
Oh, hello, Max.
Oops. I'm sorry, Dr. Early. I didn't realize you were with a patient.
It's okay, Max. You can stay.

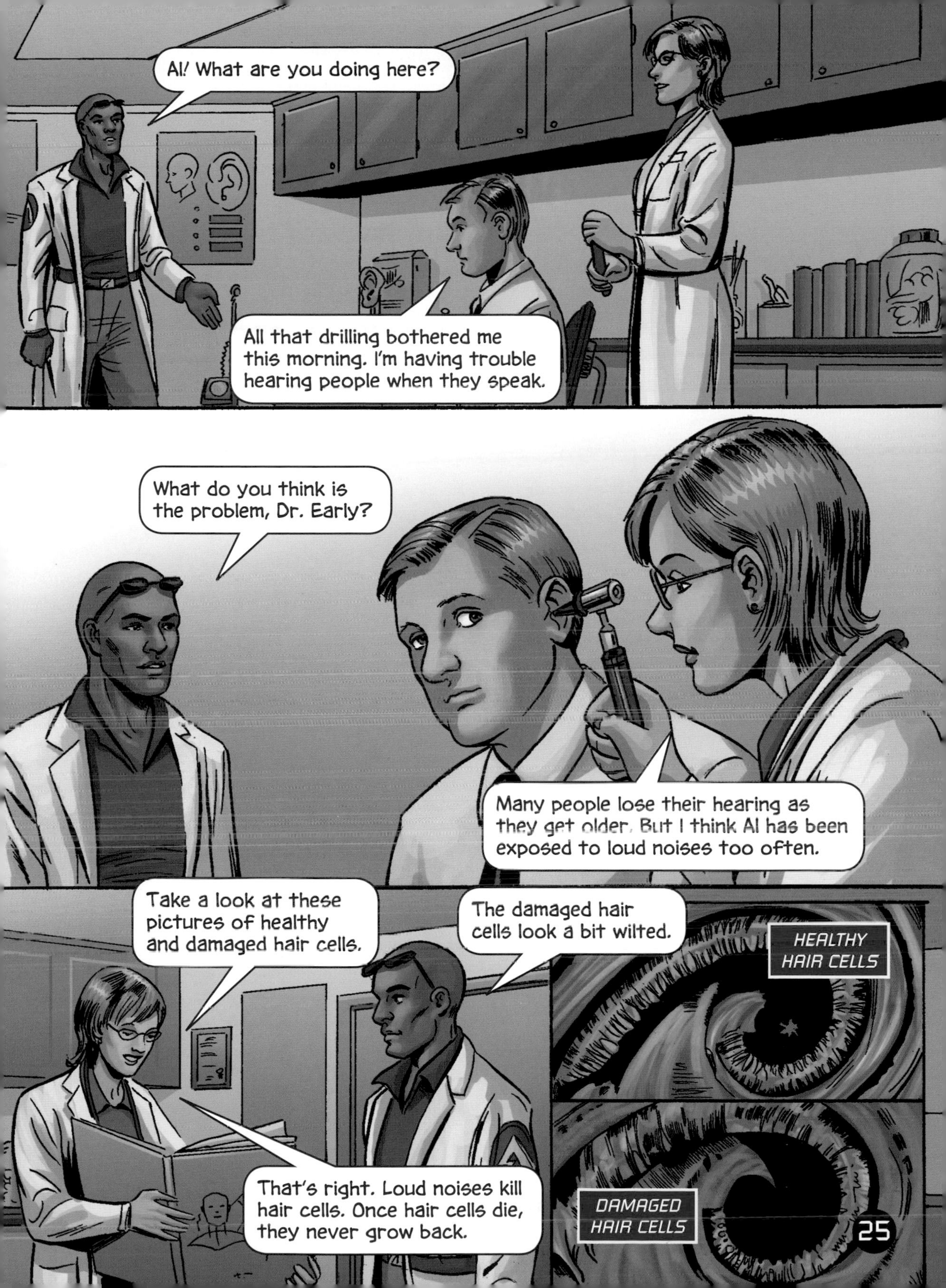
Al! What are you doing here?
All that drilling bothered me this morning. I'm having trouble hearing people when they speak.
What do you think is the problem, Dr. Early?
Many people lose their hearing as they get older. But I think Al has been exposed to loud noises too often.
Take a look at these pictures of healthy and damaged hair cells.
The damaged hair cells look a bit wilted.
HEALTHY HAIR CELLS
DAMAGED HAIR CELLS
That's right. Loud noises kill hair cells. Once hair cells die, they never grow back.

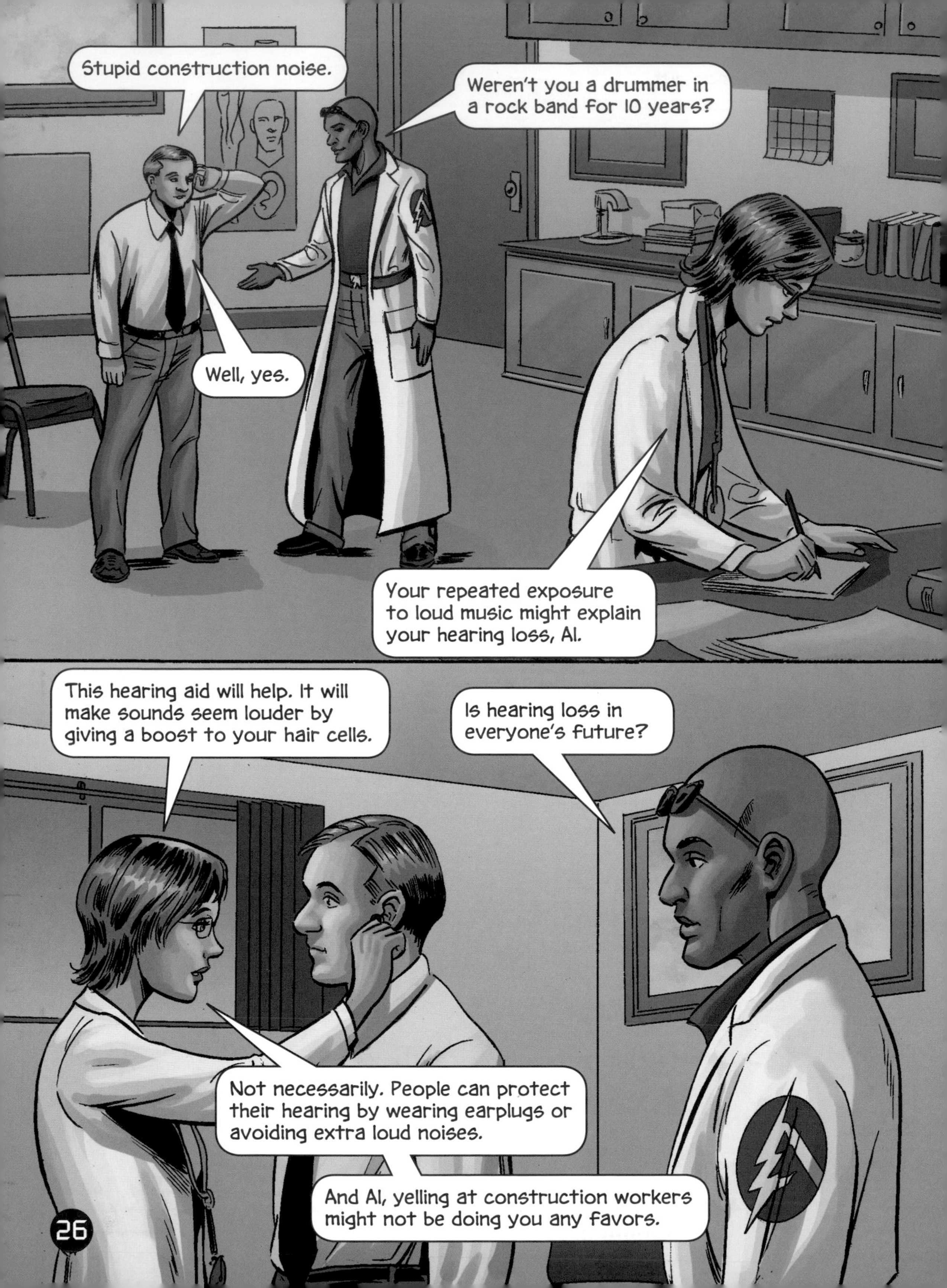
Stupid construction noise.
Weren't you a drummer in a rock band for 10 years?
Well, yes.
Your repeated exposure to loud music might explain your hearing loss, Al.
This hearing aid will help. It will make sounds seem louder by giving a boost to your hair cells.
Is hearing loss in everyone's future?
Not necessarily. People can protect their hearing by wearing earplugs or avoiding extra loud noises.
And Al, yelling at construction workers might not be doing you any favors.

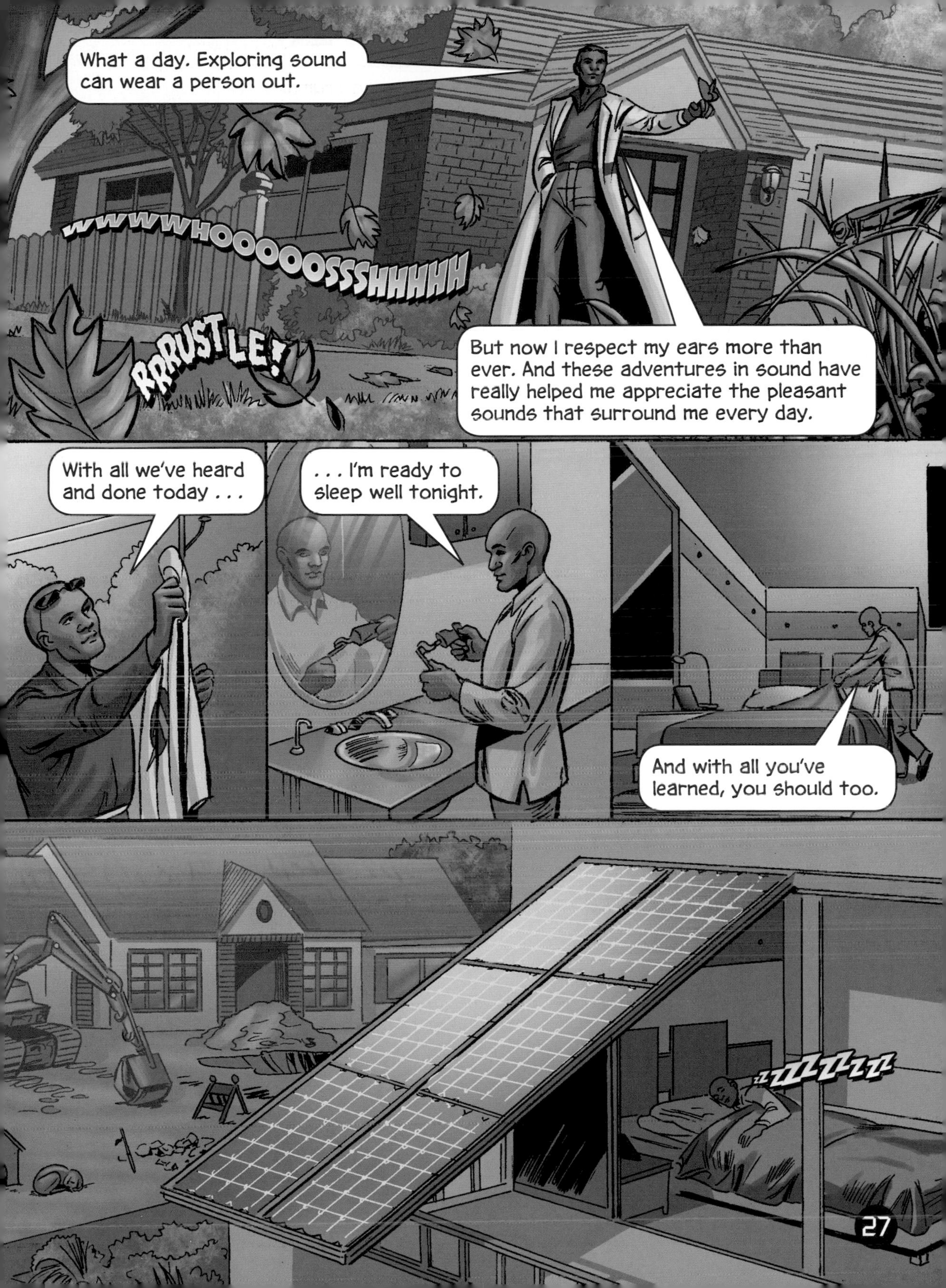
What a day. Exploring sound can wear a person out.
WWWWHOOOOOOSSSHHHHH
RRRUSTLE!
But now I respect my ears more than ever. And these adventures in sound have really helped me appreciate the pleasant sounds that surround me every day.
With all we've heard and done today . . .
. . . I'm ready to sleep well tonight.
And with all you've learned, you should too.
ZZZZZZZZ

Sound travels faster through solids than through gases and liquids. Why? Because the molecules in solids are packed closer together. The closer the molecules, the faster the sound waves travel from one molecule to the next. A sound travels 770 miles (1,239 kilometers) per hour through air. It speeds through steel at about 11,630 miles (18,716 kilometers) per hour.

 Most bats use echolocation to hunt. As they fly, bats release high pitched sounds that bounce off objects all around them. Based on the echoes they hear, the bats can locate and determine the size of insects fluttering nearby.

 The hammer, anvil, and stirrup are the smallest bones in the human body. They are the same size now as they were the day you were born. All together, they could fit on a penny.

 Ear wax helps keep your ears clean. As wax forms inside the ear canal, it clings to dirt particles. Eventually, the wax works its way out of the ear, carrying the dirt along with it.

 The liquid in the cochlea does more than just magnify vibrations. It also plays a role in balance and helps your body know what is up and what is down.

Elephants use infrasound, or sound below the range of human hearing, to talk to each other. They can use rumbling sounds as low as 5 Hz to communicate.

A cricket's hearing organs are located just below the knees of its front legs. A cicada's hearing organ is on its abdomen.

Scientists measure the loudness, or volume, of sounds in decibels (dB). A whisper measures about 20 dB, while normal talking is 60 dB. A jet measures about 120 dB and a firecracker exploding is about 140 dB. Any sound above 85 dB can cause hearing damage if listened to for too long. At close range, noise levels above 140 dB cause immediate hearing damage.

SHOEBOX GUITAR

Before you headline a world tour, jam out on this DIY guitar and learn all about the magic world of sound!

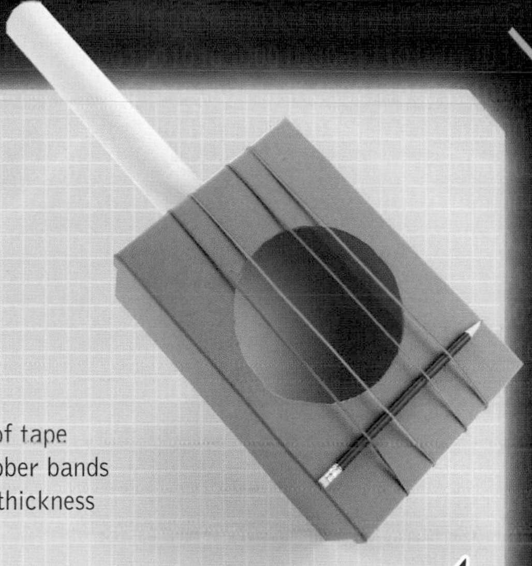

WHAT YOU NEED:

- pencil
- shoebox
- scissors
- cardboard paper towel tube
- large roll of tape
- 4 large rubber bands of various thickness

WHAT YOU DO:

1. Use the pencil to punch a hole in the center of one short side on the shoebox. Place one end of the paper towel tube over the hole and trace around it with the pencil.

2. Cut out the circle traced in step 1. Use the hole you punched to start the scissors.

3. Insert the paper towel tube into the hole. Tape the paper towel tube in place to complete the guitar's handle.

4. Use the pencil to punch a hole in the center of the shoebox's top. Draw a large circle around the hole. You may trace the roll of tape as a guide.

5. Cut out the large circle. Use the hole you punched to start the scissors.

6. Wrap the rubber bands around the shoebox lengthwise. Place them in order from widest to thinnest and space them evenly over the large hole.

7. Slide the pencil under the rubber bands just below the hole to create a bridge for the guitar strings.

8. Strum the strings to play the guitar. Try changing the angle of the bridge and the tightness of the rubber bands to make different sounds.

DISCUSSION QUESTIONS

1. How do the frequencies of high-pitch and low-pitch sounds compare in terms of the number of waves that pass by each second? Discuss the differences and think of two examples of each type of sound.

2. Thunder and lightning always happen together because they are caused by the same electrical event in the atmosphere. Why do you think we always see lightning before we hear the accompanying thunder?

3. What happens when a sound meets a surface or a new material? Discuss three possible things that can happen and explain why they occur.

4. Why is it important for a worker at a construction site to wear ear protection? Discuss your reasons.

WRITING PROMPTS

1. What is sound? Based on what you've read in this book, write a definition for sound in your own words.

2. Sound travels through air, water, and empty space at different speeds. Write a short paragraph explaining why this is the case.

3. Sound travels from a vibrating object and into your ear. Make a list of the parts of the ear the sound must pass through in order for you to hear it.

4. Bats use sonar to find their food. Draw a diagram of a bat detecting an insect with sound waves that helps explain why this ability is called echolocation.

TAKE A QUIZ! ⭐

GLOSSARY

absorb (ab-ZORB)—to soak up

cochlea (KOH-klee-uh)—a spiral-shaped part of the ear that helps send sound messages to the brain

decibel (DESS-uh-bel)—a unit for measuring the volume of sounds

eardrum (IHR-druhm)—a thin piece of skin stretched tight like a drum inside the ear; the eardrum vibrates when sound waves strike it.

echolocation (eh-koh-loh-KAY-shuhn)—the process of using sounds and echoes to locate objects; bats use echolocation to find food.

energy (EN-ur-jee)—the ability to do work, such as moving things or giving heat or light

frequency (FREE-kwuhn-see)—the number of sound waves that pass a location in a certain amount of time

hertz (HURTS)—a unit for measuring the frequency of sound wave vibrations; one hertz equals one sound wave per second.

molecule (MOL-uh-kyool)—two or more atoms of the same or different elements that have bonded; a molecule is the smallest part of a compound that can be divided without a chemical change.

pitch (PICH)—the highness or lowness of a sound; low pitches have low frequencies and high pitches have high frequencies.

reflect (ri-FLEKT)—to bounce off an object

refract (ri-FRACT)—to bend when passing through a material at an angle

vibration (vye-BRAY-shuhn)—a fast movement back and forth

READ MORE

Johnson, Robin. *The Science of Sound Waves*. Catch a Wave. New York: Crabtree Publishing Company, 2018.

Oxlade, Chris. *Super Science Light and Sound Experiments: 10 Amazing Experiment With Step-by-Step Photographs*. Thaxted, England, Miles Kelly Publishing, 2016.

Spilsbury, Richard. *Investigating Sound*. Investigating Science Challenge. New York: Crabtree Publishing Company, 2018.

Use Facthound to find Internet sites related to this book.

Visit *www.facthound.com*

Just type in 9781543529449 and go!

Super-cool **stuff!** Check out projects, games and lots more at **www.capstonekids.com**